Science Notes

Dona Herweck Rice

Publishing Credits

Rachelle Cracchiolo, M.S.Ed., *Publisher*
Conni Medina, M.A.Ed., *Managing Editor*
Nika Fabienke, Ed.D., *Content Director*
Véronique Bos, *Creative Director*
Shaun N. Bernadou, *Art Director*
Valerie Morales, *Associate Editor*
John Leach, *Assistant Editor*
Courtney Roberson, *Senior Graphic Designer*

Image Credits: p.4 Sciencephotos/Alamy; p.6 Gary Gladstone/Getty Images; p.8 PA Images/Alamy; p.9 Jeff Moore/Splash News/Newscom; all other images from iStock and/or Shutterstock.

Library of Congress Cataloging-in-Publication Data

Names: Rice, Dona, author.
Title: Science notes / Dona Herweck Rice.
Description: Huntington Beach, CA : Teacher Created Materials, [2019] | Audience: K to grade 3. |
Identifiers: LCCN 2018029724 (print) | LCCN 2018029831 (ebook) | ISBN 9781493899210 | ISBN 9781493898473
Subjects: LCSH: Science--Methodology--Juvenile literature. | Vocabulary.
Classification: LCC Q175.2 (ebook) | LCC Q175.2 .R52945 2019 (print) | DDC 507.2/1--dc23
LC record available at https://lccn.loc.gov/2018029724

Teacher Created Materials
5301 Oceanus Drive
Huntington Beach, CA 92649-1030
www.tcmpub.com

ISBN 978-1-4938-9847-3
© 2019 Teacher Created Materials, Inc.
Printed in China
Nordica.082018.CA21800936

They write words about the  .

plants

They write words about the .

ocean

They write words about the .

rocks

They write words

about the .

fossils

They write words about the .

rain

They write words about the .

clouds

They write words about the .

penguins

They write words about the .

monkeys

They write words about the .

water

They write words about the  .

stars

High-Frequency Words

New Words

about   words

write

Review Words

the   they